Usborne Essential Spanish Phrases

Nicole Irving & Leslie Colvin

Illustrated by Ann Johns

Language consultants: Isabel Sánchez Gallego, Graciella Edo de
Grigg, Marión Lorente Moltó and Margarita Díaz Gutiérrez

Edited by Megan Cullis
Series editor: Sue Meredith

This edition first published in 2009 by Usborne Publishing Ltd.,
Usborne House, 83-85 Saffron Hill, London EC1N 8RT, England.
www.usborne.com

Printed in Dubai, UAE.

Usborne Quicklinks

The Usborne Quicklinks Website is packed with links to all the best
websites on the internet. For links to some great websites to help
you learn Spanish, go to **www.usborne-quicklinks.com** and enter
the keywords: "essential spanish"

When using the internet please follow the internet safety guidelines
displayed on the Usborne Quicklinks Website.

The recommended websites in Usborne Quicklinks are regularly
reviewed and updated, but Usborne Publishing Ltd. is not
responsible for the content or availability of any website other
than its own. We recommend that children are
supervised while using the internet.

Contents

4   About the phrasebook
5   Absolute essentials
6   Asking the way
8   Travel: trains, underground, buses
10   Travel: air, sea, taxis
11   Travel: on the road
12   Accommodation: places to stay
13   Accommodation: hotels
14   Accommodation: staying with people
16   Banks, post offices, phones
18   Cafés
20   Eating out
22   Eating in
24   Shopping
27   Shopping: food
28   Shopping: clothes
30   Music
32   Going out: making arrangements, sightseeing
34   Films, TV, books
36   Talking about yourself
38   Other people
40   Sports
44   Studying
46   Interests and issues
48   Illness, problems, emergencies
50   Slang and everyday Spanish
52   Countries, nationalities, faiths
53   Numbers, colours, days, dates
54   Time, seasons, weather, fact file: Spain and South America
55   Spanish pronunciation
56   How Spanish works
61   Word list
64   Index

About the phrasebook

This book gives simple, up-to-date Spanish to help you survive, travel and socialize in Spain. It also gives basic information about Spain and tips for low budget travellers.

Finding the right words

Use the Contents list on page 3 to find the section of the book you need. If you don't find a phrase where you expect it to be, try a related section. There are food words, for example, on several pages. If you still can't find the word, try looking it up in the word list at the back.

Go for it

Remember that you can make yourself clear with very few words, or words that are not quite right. Saying "¿Madrid?" while pointing at a train will provoke *sí* or *no* (yes or no). The Spanish listed on the opposite page is absolutely essential.

You will feel more confident if you have some idea of how to pronounce Spanish correctly and of how the language works. If Spanish is new to you, try looking through the sections on pages 55-60. A good pronunciation tip is to make your voice go up at the end of a question. This will help it to sound different from a statement.

Being polite

Words like *por favor* (please) or *gracias* (thank you) make anything sound more polite and will generally guarantee a friendly response.

There are other ways of being polite in Spanish. The words *Señor* (Sir) and *Señora* (Madam) are often used to address older people whose names you don't know.

Spanish has four words for "you". You say *tú* to a friend and *vosotros/vosotras* to friends. *Usted* is polite and used for an older person or someone you don't know. *Ustedes* is the plural polite form. You can find out more about these forms on page 57. Using *tú* or *vosotros/vosotras* to people who don't expect it can be very rude. In this book the most appropriate form has been used, according to the occasion. Sometimes you will have to judge whether polite or informal is best, so both are given. If you are ever in doubt, use the polite form.

The language in this book is everyday, spoken Spanish, ranging from the formal to the colloquial. An asterisk after a Spanish word shows that it is slang or fairly familiar, e.g. *los viejos** (parents).

Masculine or feminine?

Adjectives with two forms in Spanish are given twice, e.g. red – *rojo/roja*. The first is masculine (m) and the second is feminine (f). You can find out more about masculine and feminine in Spanish on page 56.

Questions

In written Spanish you put an upside down question mark at the start of a question and a standard one at the end, e.g. *¿Quieres comer?* (Do you want to eat?)

¡Perdone! Nos hemos perdido.
Excuse me, we're lost.

¿Dónde van?
Where are you going?

Absolute essentials

yes	sí
no	no
maybe	quizás
I don't know.	No sé.
I don't mind.	No me importa.
please	por favor
thank you	gracias
excuse me	perdone[1]/perdona[2]
sorry	perdone[1]/perdona[2]
I'm very sorry.	Lo siento mucho.
not at all	de nada
hello, hi	hola
goodbye, bye	adiós
see you, bye	hasta la vista
see you later	hasta luego
good morning	buenos días
good evening	buenas tardes
good night	buenas noches
see you soon	hasta pronto
How are things?	¿Qué tal?
Mr., Sir	señor
Mrs., Madam	señora
Miss	señorita
and	y
or	o
when?	¿cuándo?
where is?	¿dónde?
why?	¿por qué?
because	porque
how?	¿cómo?
how much?	¿cuánto?
How much is it?	¿Cuánto cuesta?
What is it/this?	¿Qué es esto?
it is	es
this is	esto es
is there?	¿hay?
there is	hay
I'd like	Quisiera[1]/Quiero[2]

Getting help with Spanish

I don't understand.
No comprendo/entiendo.

Can you write it down?
¿Puede escribirlo?

Can you say that again?
¿Puede repetir?

A bit slower, please.
Un poco más despacio, por favor.

What does this word mean?
¿Qué significa esta palabra?

What's the Spanish for this?
¿Como se dice esto en español?

Have you got a dictionary?
¿Tiene un diccionario?

Do you speak English?
¿Habla inglés?

Más despacio, por favor.
Slower, please.

Signs you may see

Salida de emergencia	Emergency exit
¡Cuidado!	Beware!
¡Cuidado con el perro!	Beware of the dog!
Prohibido el paso	Keep out, no entry
Prohibido fumar	No smoking
Propriedad privada	Private property
¡Peligro!	Danger!
Agua potable	Drinking water
Prohibido nadar	No swimming

¿Está María, por favor?
Is Maria there please?

[1] Polite form. [2] Familiar form.

Asking the way

Fact file

You will find an *Oficina de Información y Turismo* (tourist office) in most big towns and cities. In tourist areas even small towns have one. Opening times are usually 9-1 and 3.30-6 on weekdays and 9-1 on Saturday. Most tourist offices provide town plans and leaflets on local sights free of charge. They also give advice on places to stay and travel arrangements. They often employ someone who speaks English.

Go straight ahead.
Siga todo recto.

It's on the left/right.
Está a la izquierda/derecha.

Follow the signs for Cadiz.
Siga las señales para Cádiz.

Go left/right.
Vaya a la izquierda/derecha.

Take the first on the left.
Tome la primera a la izquierda.

Take the second turning on the right.
Tome la segunda bocacalle a la derecha.

It's...	Está...
Go...	Vaya...
Carry on...	Siga...
straight ahead	todo recto
Turn...	Gire... Tuerza...
left	izquierda
right	derecha
Take...	Tome...
the first	la primera
the second	la segunda
the third	la tercera
the fourth	la cuarta
turning	la bocacalle
crossroads, junction	el cruce
roundabout	la glorieta
traffic lights	el semáforo
pedestrian crossing	el paso de peatones
subway	el paso subterráneo
Cross...	Cruce...
Follow...	Siga...
street	la calle
road	la carretera
main...	...principal
path	la senda, el camino
square	la plaza
motorway	la autopista

ringroad	la carretera de circunvalación
one way	dirección única
no entry	dirección prohibida
no parking	prohibido aparcar
car park	el aparcamiento
parking meters	los parquímetros
pedestrian area	la zona peatonal
pedestrians	los peatones
pavement	la acera
town centre	el centro de la ciudad
area, part of town	el barrio
outskirts, suburbs	las afueras
town hall	el ayuntamiento
bridge	el puente
river	el río
park	el parque
post office	la oficina de correos
shops	las tiendas
church	la iglesia
school	el colegio, la escuela
museum	el museo
railway line	la vía del tren
just before the	justo antes de
just after the	justo después de
at the end	al final
on the corner	en la esquina
next to	al lado de
opposite	enfrente de
in front of	delante de
behind	detrás de
above	encima, por encima
beneath	bajo, debajo de
over	sobre
under	debajo de
in	en, dentro de
on	en, encima de
here	aquí
there	allí
over there	por allí
far	lejos
close, near	cerca
nearby, near here	cerca de aquí
around here	por aquí
somewhere	en alguna parte
in this area	en esta zona
l0 minutes walk	a diez minutos a pie
5 minutes drive	a cinco minutos en coche
on foot	a pie

¿Cómo se va al camping?
What's the best way to the campsite?

¿Puede indicármelo en el mapa?
Can you show me on the map?

¿Dónde está la playa más cercana?
Where's the nearest beach?

¿Queda muy lejos?
Is it far?

¿Por dónde se va al albergue juvenil?
How do I get to the youth hostel?

Travel: trains, underground, buses

Getting information

¿A qué hora sale el próximo tren a Madrid?
What time is the next train to Madrid?

¿Cuánto dura el viaje?
How long is the journey?

¿Tengo que cambiar de tren?
Do I have to change?

Fact file

For getting around Spain, *autobuses interurbanos* (long-distance buses) are a good option as they are frequent, cheap and go to remote places. There are many bus companies, and buses to the same destination may leave from different places. For information, try the tourist office, bus station or, in a small place, a bar. Get tickets at the bus station or on the bus.

RENFE (Spanish railways) runs a complicated train service.

The standard trains are *Exprés* and *Rápido*. *Talgo, Ter* and *AVE* are faster and more pricey. Buy tickets in advance to save confusion over which supplements you have to pay. Fares are cheaper on off-peak *días azules* (blue days). There are a few private railway companies – details from tourist offices.

Some cities have a *metro*, but they all have *autobuses urbanos* (city buses). Ten ticket booklets, e.g. *Bono-bus*, work out cheaper – available from *estancos* (tobacconists). There's little public transport on Sundays.

¿Dónde tengo que cambiar para ir al Retiro?
Where do I change for el Retiro?

¿Qué acaban de decir por el altavoz?
What did they just say over the loudspeaker?

¿De qué andén sale el tren para Sol?
Which platform for Sol?

Tickets

¿Dónde puedo comprar un billete?
Where can I buy a ticket?

Quisiera un billete de ida a Granada.
Could I have a single to Granada?

¿Hacen algún tipo de descuento?
Can I get a reduction?

¿Cómo funciona esta máquina?
How does this machine work?

I'd like to reserve a seat.	Quisiera hacer una reserva.	**ticket machine**	la máquina
railway station	la estación de tren	**student fare**	la tarifa de estudiante
underground station	la estación de metro	**ticket...**	un billete...
bus station	la estación de autobuses	**a single**	...de ida
		a return	...de ida y vuelta
bus stop	la parada de autobús	**supplement**	el suplemento
train	el tren	**left luggage locker**	la consigna automática
underground train	el metro	**map**	un mapa
tram	el tranvía	**timetable**	un horario
bus, coach	el autobús	**arrivals/departures**	llegadas/salidas
leaves at 2 o'clock	sale a las dos	**long distance**	largo recorrido
arrives at 4:30	llega a las cuatro y media	**local, suburban**	cercanías
first	primero/primera	**every day, daily**	diario
last	último/última	**weekdays and Saturdays**	laborables
next	próximo/próxima	**Sundays and holidays**	domingos y festivos
cheapest	más barato/barata	**in summer-time**	en verano
ticket office	la taquilla, la ventanilla	**out of season**	fuera de temporada
		except	excepto

Buses

¿De dónde sale el autobús para Valencia?
Where does the bus for Valencia leave from?

¿Este autobús va a Barcelona?
Is this the right bus for Barcelona?

¿Puede decirme cuándo tengo que bajar?
Can you tell me when I should get off?

Travel: air, sea, taxis

Quisiera confirmar mi vuelo.
I'd like to confirm my flight.

¿A qué hora debo presentarme?
What time should I get there?

¿Dónde tengo que facturar el equipaje?
Where do I check in?

Fact file

Airports and ports often have signs and announcements in English. There's usually a bus or train from the airport into town.

Taxis are cheap with metered fares, but it's wise to ask what the fare will be first. Taxis usually take up to four passengers. They charge extra at night, on Sundays and for large bags.

Mi equipaje no ha llegado.
My luggage hasn't arrived.

Tenía que encontrarme con la Señora Serra.
Mrs Serra is supposed to be meeting me.

Where is the taxi stand?
¿Dónde está la parada de taxis?

Take me to...
A...

What's the fare to...?
¿Cuánto costaría ir a...?

Please drop me here...
Pare aquí por favor...

airport	el aeropuerto
aeroplane	el avión
flight	vuelo
port	el puerto
ferry	el barco
(sea) crossing	travesía
I feel sea sick	Estoy mareado/ mareada
on board	a bordo
Mediterranean	Mediterráneo
suitcase	la maleta
backpack/rucksack	la mochila
bag	una bolsa
hand luggage	el equipaje de mano
trolley	el carrito
information	información
customs	la aduana
passport	el pasaporte
departure gate	la puerta de salida
boarding pass	la tarjeta de embarque
No smoking	No fumador
travel agent	una agencia de viajes
airline ticket	un billete de avión
cut price	de precio reducido
standby	aviso
charter flight	un vuelo charter
flight number	el número de vuelo
a booking	una reserva
to change	cambiar
to cancel	cancelar
a delay	un retraso

Fact file

Bikes and mopeds are often available for hire in tourist areas. You can ride mopeds from age 15, but make sure you are insured. It is illegal not to wear a crash helmet.

Remember the Spanish drive on the right. Drivers must always carry their driving licence with them. Theft from cars is a problem in some areas, so keep your documents with you and your things well out of sight.

Se me ha averiado el coche.
I've broken down.

¿Dónde está el taller más cercano?
Where's the nearest garage?

Fill it up, please.
Lleno, por favor.

I have a puncture.
Se me ha pinchado una rueda.

The engine won't start.
El motor no arranca.

The battery's flat.
La batería está descargada.

How much will it cost?
¿Cuánto costará?

for hire
de alquiler

Can I hire...?
¿Alquilan...?

Where are you going?
¿A dónde vas?

I'm going to Cadiz.
Voy a Cádiz.

town centre	centro de la ciudad
give way	ceder el paso
toll	peaje
insurance	el seguro
driving licence	el carnet de conducir
(car) documents	los papeles
petrol station	una gasolinera
petrol	la gasolina
lead-free petrol	gasolina sin plomo
oil/petrol mixture	mezcla de aceite y gasolina
garage, repair shop	un taller
oil	el aceite
litre	un litro
car	un coche
bicycle	una bicicleta
moped	una motocicleta
motorbike	una moto
crash helmet	un casco
radiator	el radiador
lights	las luces
chain	la cadena
wheel	la rueda
gears	las marchas
cable	el cable
pump	una bomba
tyre	el neumático

Los frenos no funcionan.
The brakes don't work.

No sé por qué no funciona.
I don't know what's wrong.

¿Puede repararlo usted?
Can you fix it?

Accommodation: places to stay

At the tourist office

¿Tienen una lista de campings?
Do you have a list of campsites?

Fact file

The *Oficina de Información y Turismo* (tourist office) will supply lists of places to stay. Cheap accomodation includes: *fondas* – rooms, often above a bar; *casas de huespedes* – guest houses; *pensiones* – rooms, price may include food; *hostales* – cheap hotels. You might also see signs for *camas* (beds), *habitaciones* (rooms) and *camas y comidas* (beds and meals) advertised in private houses or above bars.

Camping

Fact file

Campings (campsites) vary in price and quality and can be crowded in summer.

Is there a campsite around here?
¿Hay un camping por aquí?

Where are the showers?
¿Dónde están las duchas?

tent	una tienda
caravan	una caravana
hot water	agua caliente
cold water	agua fría
drinking water	agua potable
camping gas	camping gas
tent peg	una estaca
mallet	un mazo
sleeping bag	un saco de dormir
torch	una linterna
a box of matches	una caja de cerillas
loo paper	el papel higiénico
can opener	un abrelatas

¿Tienen sitio para acampar?
Do you have a space?

Somos tres personas con una tienda.
There are three of us with a tent.

¿Hay alguna tienda?
Do you have a shop?

¿Es potable el agua del grifo?
Is it OK to drink the tap water?

Hotels

> *¿Tienen una habitación libre?*
> **Do you have a room?**

> *El hotel está completo.*
> **We're full.**

> *¿Hay otro hotel por aquí?*
> **Is there another hotel nearby?**

> *¿Cuánto cuesta una habitación por noche?*
> **How much for a room?**

Fact file

It is advisable to make a reservation for a hotel. When you arrive, you may need to show a passport or identity card to register. In some hotels, the room has a safe *(caja fuerte)*.

> *¿El precio incluye el desayuno?*
> **Does that include breakfast?**

> *¿Puedo ver la habitación?*
> **Can I see the room?**

Rooms to let
Habitaciones

There are three of us.
Somos tres personas.

How many nights?
¿Cuántas noches?

How much do you want to pay?
¿Cuánto quiere pagar?

Can I leave a message for someone?
¿Puedo dejar un mesaje para alguien?

Can I have my passport back?
¿Puede devolverme el pasaporte?

one/two night(s)
room
  single
  double
  with three beds
clean
cheap
expensive
lunch
dinner (evening)
key
room number

una/dos noche(s)
una habitación...
...individual
...doble
...triple
limpio/limpia
barato/barata
caro/cara
la comida
la cena
la llave
el número de habitación

> *Busco una habitación para dos.*
> **I'm looking for a room for two people.**

> *¿Puede reservarme una habitación?*
> **Can you book a room for me?**

Accommodation: staying with people

Greetings

¡Hola!
Hello.

¿Como estás?
How are you?

¿Dónde puedo dejar mis cosas?
Where can I put my things?

¿Dónde voy a dormir?
Where am I sleeping?

¿A qué hora desayunáis?[1]
What time do you have breakfast?

¿Puedes despertarme a las siete?[2]
Could you wake me up at seven?

For more polite or formal greetings, use the expression most appropriate to the time of day followed by *Señor* or *Señora* (see page 4). Also use the polite form *¿Como está?* (How are you?)

Washing

¿Cómo funciona la ducha?
How does the shower work?

Is it OK to have a bath?
¿Puedo bañarme?
Do you mind if I wash a few things?
¿Puedo lavar algo de ropa?
Where can I dry these?
¿Dónde puedo secar esto?

bathroom	el cuarto de baño
bath	el baño
shower	la ducha
toilet	los servicios
loo	el lavabo
towel	una toalla
soap	jabón
shampoo	el champú
toothpaste	el dentrífrico
toothbrush	el cepillo de dientes
deodorant	el desodorante
hairdryer	el secador
hairbrush	el cepillo para el pelo
washing powder	jabón en polvo

1 To be polite, when speaking to a stranger or an older person, say *¿A qué hora desayunan?*
2 To be polite, *¿Puede despertarme a las siete?*

Being polite

¿Puedo ayudar a pagar los gastos?
Can I pay my share?

No, no te preocupes.
No, it's OK.

Gracias por hospedarme.
It's nice of you to let me stay.

No hay problema.
No problem.

alarm clock	un despertador
on the floor	en el suelo
an extra...	otro/otra...
blanket	manta
quilt, duvet	edredón
sheet	sábana
pillow	almohada
electric socket	un enchufe
T.V.	la tele
needle	una aguja
thread	el hilo
scissors	unas tijeras
iron	una plancha
upstairs	arriba
downstairs	abajo
cupboard	un armario
bedroom	el dormitorio
living room	la sala de estar
kitchen	la cocina
garden	el jardín
terrace	la terraza
balcony	el balcón

I'm tired.
Estoy cansado/cansada.

I'm knackered.
Estoy muerto/muerta de cansancio.

I'm cold.
Tengo frío.

I'm hot.
Tengo calor.

Can I have a key?
¿Puede darme una llave?

What is there to do in the evenings?
¿Qué se puede hacer por las noches aquí?

Where's the nearest phone box?
¿Dónde está la cabina más próxima?

¿Puedo llamar por teléfono?
Can I use your phone?

¿Cuánto cuesta llamar a Gran Bretaña?
How much is it to call Britain?

Pagaré la llamada.
I'll pay for the call.

Saying goodbye

Muchas gracias por todo.
Thank you for everything.

¡Adiós!
Goodbye.

15

Banks, post offices, phones

Banks

Quisiera
cambiar esto.
I want to change this.

¿Aceptan
cheques de viaje?
**Do you accept traveller's
cheques?**

¿Puedo ver su
pasaporte?
**Can I see your
passport?**

Post office

¿Me da un sello
para esta carta?
**Can I have a stamp
for this?**

¿Dónde está el
buzón más cercano?
**Where's the nearest
postbox?**

Fact file

The unit of currency is the euro (EUR). One euro is divided into 100 eurocents. Banks open 8.30-2 on weekdays, 9-1 on Saturday (not always in summer). You can change money elsewhere (look for the sign *cambio*) but you may get a poorer exchange rate. There's a good system of cashpoints. Most take foreign cashpoint cards.

Money problems

He perdido mis
cheques de viaje.
**I've lost my traveller's
cheques.**

Los números de
serie eran...
**The serial numbers
were...**

¿Cómo puedo
obtener cheques de
repuesto?
**How do I get
replacements?**

Estoy esperando un
envío de dinero, ¿ha llegado?
**I'm expecting some money,
has it arrived?**

bank	el banco
cashier's desk, till	la caja
foreign exchange	cambio
enquiries	información
money	el dinero
small change	el suelto
traveller's cheques	unos cheques de viaje
credit card	una tarjeta de crédito
commission	la comisión
money transfer	una transferencia
post office	la oficina de Correos
postcard	una postal
letter	una carta
parcel	un paquete
envelope	un sobre
by airmail	por avión
registered letter	una carta certificada
stamp	un sello
telephone	un teléfono
telephone box	una cabina de teléfono
mobile phone	un teléfono móvil
phone charger	cargador de móvil
directory	una guía telefónico
phone number	el número de teléfono
wrong number	el número equivocado

reverse charge call	una llamada a cobro revertido
Hang on.	Un momento.

The cashpoint machine (ATM) has swallowed my card.
El cajero se ha tragado mi tarjeta.

Where can I send an e-mail?
¿Dónde puedo enviar un e-mail?

What is the exchange rate?
¿A cómo está el cambio?

Fact file

Most of the payphones on the street take coins. For international calls look for the sign *Teléfono Internacional*. You can also phone from bars, department stores or a *Telefónica*. These phones are metered and you pay after the call.

You can buy stamps in a post office or an *estanco* (tobacconist).

Phones

Este teléfono no funciona.
This phone doesn't work.

¿Es éste el prefijo de Barcelona?
Is this the code for Barcelona?

Hola. ¿Está María?
Hello, is Maria there?

Por favor, dígale que he llamado.
Please tell her/him I called.

¿Cuándo volverá?
When will she be back?

¿Podría decirle que me llame?
Can she/he call me back?

Mi número es...
My number is...

¿Puedo dejar un recado para...?
Can I leave a message for...?

Cafés

café	el café
bar	el bar
table	una mesa
Cheers!	¡Salud!
something to drink	algo de beber
something to eat	algo de comer
snack	un bocado
black coffee	un café solo
white coffee	un café con leche
decaffeinated	descafeinado
tea (with milk)	un té (con leche)
hot chocolate	un chocolate caliente
fruit juice	un zumo
orange juice	un zumo de naranja
coke	una coca-cola
mineral water	un agua mineral
still	sin gas
sparkling	con gas
beer (bottled)	una cerveza
beer (draught)	una caña
glass of red wine	un vino tinto
bottle of...	botella de...
half a bottle of white wine	media botella de vino blanco
sugar	el azúcar
with ice	con hielo
slice of lemon	una rodaja de limón
olives	unas aceitunas
omelette	una tortilla
cheese sandwich	un sandwich de queso
ham (cured)	jamón serrano
ham (cooked)	jamón de York
ice cream	un helado

Fact file

There is little difference between a Spanish bar, café and *cafetería*. Most of them open 9.30am to 11pm. Prices vary (smart means pricey). If you sit down, a waiter serves you but everything is cheaper at the bar.

Look out for *tapas* (starter-like dishes), see page 21. Other snacks include *churros* (doughnuts), *omelettes* (*española* has potato, *francesa* is plain) and sandwiches.

¿Vamos a tomar un café?
How about a coffee?

¿Está ocupada esta silla?
Is this chair free?

¿Puedo ver el menú?
Can I see the menu?

Un café solo, por favor.
A black coffee, please.

¿Tienen batidos?
Do you have milk-shakes?

Choosing a place

¿Dónde vamos?
Where shall we go?

No me gustan las pizzas.
I don't like pizzas.

Vamos a comer una hamburguesa.
Let's go for a hamburger.

Spanish food	la comida española	**fried egg**	huevo frito
Italian...	...italiana	**spaghetti**	unos espaguetis
Chinese...	...china	**rare**	muy poco hecho/hecha
cheap restaurant	un restaurante barato		
take-away (food)	para llevar	**medium**	poco hecho/hecha
menu	el menú	**well done**	muy hecho/hecha
starter	el primer plato	**mustard**	la mostaza
main course	el segundo plato	**salt**	la sal
dessert	el postre	**pepper**	la pimienta
price	el precio	**dressing**	la vinagreta
soup	la sopa	**mayonnaise**	la mayonesa
fish	el pescado		
meat	la carne		
vegetables	las verduras	**Is everything all right?**	
cheese	el queso	¿Todo bien?	
fruit	la fruta	**Yes, it's very good.**	
chips	patatas fritas	Si, está muy bueno.	
sausages	unas salchichas		
salad	ensalada		
hamburger	una hamburguesa		

Deciding what to have

¿Puede hacer uno sin queso?
Can I have one without cheese?

¿Qué es eso?
What's that?

Tomaré uno de esos.
I'll have one of those.

Problems

Yo pedí una paella.
I ordered paella.

La carne está poco hecha.
The meat isn't cooked enough.

¿No tienen ketchup?
Don't you have any ketchup?

¡Por favor!
Excuse me!

¿Puede traernos la cuenta, por favor?
Can we have the bill please?

Yo no había pedido eso.
I didn't order this.

Fact file

Spanish food is good value and well worth exploring, but to eat out cheaply you need to be adventurous – there aren't many fast-food places.

Look out for bars that serve *tapas* (snacks or starter-like dishes). These include olives, *chorizo* (spicy salami) seafood such as *gambas* (prawns) or *calamares* (squid), *habas* (beans), etc. The dishes are often on the counter so you can point to show what you want. Have one *ración* (portion) as a snack or several as a meal. Alternatively order *unos platos* (a large plateful).

Tapas are cheap, but remember that in most bars, prices are even lower if you eat at the counter.

There are lots of restaurants serving good, inexpensive food. Try *un retaurante* or, for local food, *una fonda*. Most of these display a *menú turístico* (set menu) with its price. This is usually three courses with a drink and is often good value. *El menú del día* (dish of the day) or the *platos combinados* (various dishes served on one plate) can be cheap.

Most bills say *servicio incluido* (service included) but tipping is normal practice so it's best to leave a small tip.

Fact file

Breakfast is coffee with pastries or toast. Mid-morning snacks are common. The main meal is at about 3 and it is often three courses. Soups may be cold. Water, wine and bread are always served and pudding is often fruit. The evening meal is lighter and late, at 9, 10 or even 11. On weekends, it is normal to go out before dinner for drinks and tapas. This is called: *ir de vinos* or *ir de tapas*.

Enjoy your meal.
¡Buen provecho!

I'm hungry/thirsty.
Tengo hambre/sed.

I'm not hungry/thirsty.
No tengo hambre.

Helping

¿Puedo ayudar?
Can I help?

¿Puedo poner la mesa?
Can I lay the table?

¿Puedo fregar los platos?
Can I do the washing-up?

breakfast	el desayuno	**prawns**	las gambas
lunch	la comida, el almuerzo	**tuna fish**	el atún
dinner (evening)	la cena	**hake**	la merluza
bowl	un tazón	**monkfish**	el rape
glass	el vaso	**rice**	el arroz
plate	el plato	**pasta**	la pasta
knife	un cuchillo	**potatoes**	las patatas
fork	un tenedor	**onions**	las cebollas
spoon	una cuchara	**garlic**	el ajo
bread	el pan	**tomatoes**	los tomates
jam	la mermelada	**peppers**	los pimientos
butter	la mantequilla	**peas**	los guisantes
margarine	la margarina	**aubergine**	la berenjena
chicken	un pollo	**asparagus**	los espárragos
pork	(la carne de) cerdo	**spinach**	las espinacas
beef	(la carne de) vaca	**raw**	crudo/cruda
veal	(la carne de) ternera	**(too) hot, spicy**	(demasiado) picante
liver	el hígado	**salty**	salado/salada
squid	calamares	**sweet**	dulce

Special cases

No me gusta el pescado.
I don't like fish.

Soy vegetariano[1].
I'm a vegetarian.

Soy alérgico a los huevos[2].
I'm allergic to eggs.

[1] If you're a girl, say *vegetariana*. [2] If you're a girl, say *alérgica*.

Shopping

¿Qué desea?
Can I help you?

Quisiera uno de estos.
I'd like one of these.

¿Cuánto cuesta esto?
How much is it?

Fact file

Opening times vary but bear in mind that many shops close for lunch. Shops generally open Monday to Friday 9.30 to 1.30 and 4 or 5 to 7.30 or 8, and 9.30 to 2 on Saturday. Many bakers are also open on Sunday morning.

Department stores open 10 to 8 without a break, Monday to Saturday. Look out for the sign *cerrado los* (closed on...).

An *estanco* sells stamps as well as cigarettes. A *ferretería* sells handy things for camping but try a *tienda de deportes* for camping equipment. A *farmacia* has medicines and plasters and a *perfumería* sells make-up, shampoo, soap etc. but things like this are cheaper in local supermarkets, or *supermercados*.

The best and cheapest place for food and everyday things is a *hipermercado*. These are located outside towns or inside large shopping malls, and they sell a huge range of products at low prices. Villages have at least one local bakery, or *panadería*, but there are few greengrocers. People buy their fruit and vegetables from a *tienda* or a market.

Markets are held regularly. Big towns have them daily and smaller places twice a week. They're colourful and lively as well as being good for food and local produce.

For picnic things, go to a *tienda* or buy sandwiches from a *tapas* bar (see page 21). In cities you might find a *charcutería* where you can buy sausages, salamis, ham etc.

¿Podría escribir el precio, por favor?
Please could you write down the price?

Está bien.
That's fine.

Veinte euros.
It's twenty euros.

Me lo llevo.
I'll take it.

shopping centre	el centro comercial
shop	una tienda
department store	unos grandes almacenes
market	el mercado
supermarket	un supermercado
general shop	una tienda (de comestibles)
grocer	un colmado[1]
baker	una panadería
cake shop	una pastelería
butcher	una carnicería
delicatessen	delicatessen
fruit/veg stall, greengrocer	una verdulería
fishmonger	una pescadería
healthfood shop	una tienda naturista, herboristería
hardware shop	una ferretería
chemist	una farmacia
camera shop	una tienda de fotografía
gift department	objetos de regalo
tobacconist	un estanco
news kiosk	un quiosco de periódicos
bookshop	una librería
stationer	una papelería
record shop	una tienda de discos
computer store	una tienda de ordenadores
video shop	videoclub
flea market	un rastro
junk shop	un baratillo
sports shop	una tienda de deportes
shoe shop	una zapatería
shoe mender	un zapatero
hairdresser	una peluquería
barber	un barbero
laundry	una lavandería
travel agent	una agencia de viajes
open	abierto/abierta
closed	cerrado/cerrada
entrance	la entrada
exit	la salida
check-out	la caja
stairs	una escalera
price	el precio

¿Dónde está el centro comercial?
Where's the main shopping area?

¿Venden pilas?
Do you sell batteries?

¿Dónde se puede comprar pilas?
Where can I buy batteries?

¿Dónde pueden arreglarme esto?
Where can I get this repaired?

¿Dónde hay una buena tienda de gafas de sol?
Where's a good shop for sunglasses?

[1] The word *colmado* is used in Catalonia. See page 54 for the different regions of Spain.

25

Shopping

¿Qué desea?
Can I help you?

¿Puedo ver ése?
Can I see that one?

¿Cuánto cuesta?
How much is it?

Estoy mirando.
I'm just looking.

sunscreen	una crema con protección
make-up	el maquillaje
(hair) gel	el gel fijador
mousse	el mousse
tampons	unos tampones
tissues	unos pañuelos de papel, clínex
razor	una maquinilla de afeitar
shaving foam	espuma de afeitar
contact lens solution	el líquido para lentillas
plasters	unas tiritas
film	una película
English newspapers	unos periódicos ingleses
postcard	una postal
writing paper	el papel de escribir
envelope	un sobre
notepad	una libreta
ball-point pen	un bolígrafo
pencil	un lápiz
poster	un poster
stickers	unos adhesivos
badges	unas insignias
sunglasses	unas gafas de sol
jewellery	las joyas
watch	un reloj
earrings	unos pendientes
ring	un anillo
purse	un monedero
wallet	una cartera
bag	una bolsa
smaller	más pequeño/pequeña
cheaper	más barato/barata
another colour	otro color

Quiero pensarlo un poco.
I want to think about it.

Necesito una crema bronceadora.
I need some suntan lotion.

¿Tienen una más grande?
Do you have a bigger one?

Quisiera dos panecillos.
I'd like two rolls.

¿Puede darme tres euros de uvas?
Can I have three euros worth of grapes?

¿Puede darme un poco de ese paté?
Can I have a bit of that pâté?

carrier-bag	una bolsa	**peanuts**	unos cacahuetes
small	pequeño/pequeña	**apples**	manzanas
large	grande	**pears**	peras
a slice of (meat)	una tajada	**peaches**	melocotones
a bit more	un poco más	**nectarines**	nectarinas
a bit less	un poco menos	**plums**	ciruelas
a portion	una porción	**cherries**	cerezas
a piece of	un trozo de	**strawberries**	fresas
a kilogram	un kilo	**apricots**	albaricoques
half a kilo	medio kilo	**melon**	un melón
100 grammes	cien gramos	**bananas**	plátanos
organic	orgánico	**oranges**	manzanas
bread	el pan		
stick	una barra		
round loaf	una hogaza		
wholemeal bread	pan integral		
savoury pie	una empanada		
sweets	unos dulces		
chocolate	el chocolate		
crisps	unas patatas fritas, unas papas		

Fact file

There are many different types of bread that you can try. A standard loaf is *una barra*. If you want something smaller, ask for *una barra pequeña*.

Un poco más, por favor.
A bit more please.

¿Así?
Like that?

Vale, así está bien, gracias.
OK, that's enough, thanks.

Shopping: clothes

clothes	la ropa		
shirt	una camisa		
T-shirt	una camiseta		
sweatshirt, jumper	una sudadera		
fleece	un forro polar		
dress	un vestido		
skirt	una falda		
trousers	unos pantalones		
jeans	unos vaqueros, unos tejanos		
shorts	unos pantalones cortos		
tracksuit	un chándal		
top	la parte de arriba	extra large	extra grande
bottom	la parte de abajo	too big	demasiado grande
trainers	unas zapatillas de deporte	smaller	más pequeño/pequeña
		long	largo/larga
shoes	unos zapatos	short	corto/corta
sandals	unas sandalias	tight	ceñido/ceñida
boots	unas botas	baggy	suelto/suelta
belt	un cinturón	fashion	la moda
(ski) jacket	un anorak	a look, style	un estilo
boxer shorts/pants	unos calzoncillos	fashionable	de moda
knickers	unas bragas	trendy, cool	moderno/moderna
bra	un sostén, un sujetador	out-of-date, untrendy	pasado de moda
tights	unas medias		
socks	unos calcetines	smart	elegante
swimsuit, trunks	un bañador	dressy	bien vestido/vestida
small	pequeño/pequeña	scruffy	desaliñado/desaliñada
medium	mediano/mediana	sale	las rebajas
large	grande	changing room	el probador

Fact file

For reasonably priced clothes, try hypermarkets such as *Continente*, *Alcampo* and *Carrefour*. Look out for sales: *las rebajas de inverno* (after Christmas) and *las rebajas de verano* (before the end of the summer). A well-known charity shop is *Cruz Roja* (Red Cross shop).

¿Puedo ir en vaqueros?
Are jeans all right?

¿Puedes prestarme tu chaqueta?
Can I borrow your jacket?

¿Llevo el traje de baño?
Shall I bring my swimming stuff?

Music

¿Dónde hay una buena tienda de discos?
Where's a good place to buy CDs?

Can I put some music on?
¿Puedo poner música?

I listen to (lots of)...
Escucho mucho...

Can you record this for me?
¿Puedes grabarme este disco?

Turn it up.
Sube el volumen.

It's too loud.
Está demasiado alto.

Turn it down.
Baja el volumen.

¿Tienen esto en CD?
Do you have this on CD?

¿Has visto el vídeo?
Have you seen the video?

¿Tienen una sección de jazz?
Do you have a jazz section?

¿De quién es?
Who's this by?

Playing an instrument

Do you play an instrument?
¿Tocas algún instrumento?

I play the guitar.
Toco la guitarra.

I sing in a band.
Canto en un grupo.

Which instrument do you like best?
¿Qué instrumento prefieres?

I play in a band.
Toco en un grupo.

I'm learning the drums.
Estoy aprendiendo a tocar la batería.

¿Qué tipo de música te gusta?
What kind of music do you like?

¿Has oído su último disco?
Have you heard the latest album?

¡Son malísimos!
They're useless!

¿Puedes prestarme este CD?
Can I borrow this album?

¡Es fantástico!
It's brilliant!

music	la música
music shop	una tienda de música
radio	la radio
CD	CD
CD player	un reproductor de CD
MP3 player	un reproductor de MP3
hi-fi	una cadena de alta fidelidad
headphones	unos auriculares
single	un single, un sencillo
download	descargar
blank disk	CD virgen
music video	un vídeo musical
song, track	una canción
lyrics	la letra
tune, melody	una melodía
rhythm	el ritmo
live music	música en directo
group, band	un grupo
solo artist	un solista
singer	el cantante
accompaniment	el acompañamiento
fan	un/una fan
tour	una gira
concert, gig	un concierto
the Top 40[1]	los 40 Principales
number one	el número uno
hit	un éxito
latest	último/última
new	nuevo/nueva
piano	el piano
keyboards	el teclado
electric guitar	la guitarra eléctrica
bass guitar	el bajo
saxophone	el saxofón
trumpet	la trompeta
harmonica	la armónica
violin	el violín
flute	la flauta
choir	un coro
orchestra	una orquesta

Types of music

This list includes music you're likely to hear in Spain. For other types of music, try using the English word as the names are often the same.

house music	house
heavy metal	heavy metal
rock	rock
rap	rap
hip-hop	hip-hop
techno	tecno
reggae	reggae
funk	funk
flamenco	flamenco
Afro-cuban	música afrocubana
Brazilian	musica brasileña
rock & roll	rock & roll
jazz	jazz
folk	folk
pop	pop
dance, disco	disco
classical	clásica
70's music	música de los setenta

[1] The most common pop chart in Spain is the Top 40.

Going out: making arrangements, sightseeing

Hola, ¿qué hacemos?
Hello, what's happening?

¿Tienes alguna idea?
Have you got any ideas?

¿Hacemos algo esta noche?
Shall we do something tonight?

Estoy ocupado[1].
I can't, I'm busy.

¿A qué hora?
What time?

¿Dónde quedamos?
Where shall we meet?

Nos vemos en la fuente.
See you at the fountain.

Do you know a good place to...	¿Conoces un buen sitio para...
go dancing?	ir a bailar?
listen to music?	eschuchar música?
eat?	comer?
go for a drink?	ir de copas?
nightclub	un club nocturno, una disco
disco	una discoteca
rave	un rave
party	una fiesta
picnic	un picnic, una excursión
barbecue	una barbacoa
theatre	un teatro
show, entertainment	un espectáculo
cinema	un cine
a film	una película
a performance, showing	una sesión
ballet	ballet
opera	ópera
ticket office	la taquilla
Is there an admission charge?	¿Hay que pagar entrada?
Can I get a ticket in advance?	¿Puedo comprar la entrada por anticipado?
student ticket	una entrada de estudiante
What time does it...	¿A qué hora...
start?	empieza?
finish?	acaba?
open	abre?
close?	cierra?
today	hoy
tomorrow	mañana
day after tomorrow	pasado mañana
(in the) morning	(por la) mañana
(in the) afternoon	(por la) tarde
(in the) evening	(por la) noche
this week	esta semana
next week	la próxima semana
entertainment guide	una guía de espectáculos

[1] Say *Estoy ocupada* if you're a girl.

Fact file

If you want to find out what to visit, go to the tourist office. Here you will get free maps, town plans and leaflets.

To find out what's on, most cities have listings magazines. Towns have *carteleras* (listing pages in local newspapers). Many films are dubbed but some are in *versión original* (original language) or *V.O.*

People go out late. The last film showing is at 10.30 or 11. Clubs may not fill up until 1 am.

What is there to see around here?	¿Qué se puede ver por aquí?	the old town	el centro histórico
tour	una excursión	cathedral	la catedral
region	la región	church	una iglesia
countryside	el campo	castle	un castillo
mountains	la montaña	tower	una torre
lake	el lago	city walls	las murallas
river	el río	ruins	unas ruinas
coast	la costa	caves	unas cuevas
on the beach	en la playa	theme park	el parque de atracciones
in town	en el centro		
at X's place	en casa de X	festival	el festival
museum	un museo	fireworks	los fuegos artificiales
art gallery	una galería de arte	bullfight	una corrida de toros
exhibition	una exposición	interesting	interesante
craft exhibition	una exposición de artesanía	dull, boring	aburrrido/aburrida
		beautiful	bonito/bonita

Films, TV, books

cinema	un cine	**actor/actress**	el actor, la actriz
film society/club	un club de cine	**fringe**	experimental/
theatre	un teatro		independiente
library	una biblioteca	**film buff**	un experto en cine
film, movie	una película	**production**	una producción
play	una obra de teatro	**plot**	el argumento
book	un libro	**story**	la historia
magazine	una revista	**set**	el decorado
comic	un comic	**special-effects**	los efectos especiales
novel	una novela	**photography**	la fotografía
poetry	poesía	**TV, telly**	la tele
author	el autor	**TV (silly box)**	la caja tonta*
director (film)	el director	**remote control**	el mando a distancia
cast	el reparto	**cable TV**	la televisión por cable

34

satellite TV	la televisión satélite	adventure story	una historia de aventuras
digital TV	la televisión digital	war film	una película de guerra
programme	el programa	a Western	una película del Oeste
channel	el canal	sci-fi	ciencia ficción
news	las noticias	suspense	suspense
weather	el tiempo	sex	sexo
documentary	el documental	violence	violencia
cartoons	dibujos animados	political	político/política
game show	un concurso televisivo	satirical	satírico/satírica
soap opera	la telenovela, un culebrón	serious	serio/seria
		offbeat	original
ads	los anuncios	commercial	comercial
dubbed	doblado/doblada	exciting	emocionante
in English	en inglés	over the top	exagerado/exagerada
with subtitles	con subtítulos, subtitulada	good	bueno/buena
		OK	bien
famous	famoso/famosa	bad	malo/mala
award-winning	ganador/a de un premio	lousy	malísimo/malísima
		silly	tonto/tonta
blockbuster	la película taquillera	funny, fun	divertido/divertida
a classic	un clásico	sad	triste
comedy	una comedia	scary	de miedo
thriller	thriller/una película policiaca	Where can I hire a DVD?	¿Dónde se puede alquilar un DVD?
musical	un musical	Do I have to be a member?	¿Tengo que ser socio?
horror film	una película de terror		

¿Me puedes prestar algo para leer?
Can you lend me something to read?

Leí ese libro en la escuela.
I did that book at school.

¿De qué va?
What's it about?

Es fantástico.
It's brilliant.

¿Has leído esto?
Have you read this?

Es aburridísimo.
It's so boring.

¿De quién es?
Who's it by?

¿Estás sola?
Are you alone?

¿Tienes alguna hermana?
Have you got any sisters?

¿Dónde te alojas?
Where are you staying?

No, estoy viajando con amigos.
No, I'm travelling with friends.

I'm English.
Soy inglés/inglesa.

My family is from...
Mi familia es de...

I've been here for two weeks.
Llevo dos semanas aquí.

I'm on an exchange.
He venido de intercambio.

I'm on holiday.
He venido de vacaciones.

I'm staying with friends.
Estoy en casa de unos amigos.

I am a friend of...
Soy amigo/amiga de...

I'm studying Spanish.
Estoy estudiando español.

I'm travelling around.
Estoy viajando por el país.

My parents are divorced.
Mis padres están divorciados.

My birthday is on the...
Mi cumpleaños es el (día)...

I'm an only child.
Soy hijo único/hija única.

My name is...	Me llamo...
I live...	Vivo...
in the country	en el campo
in a town	en una ciudad
in the suburbs	en las afueras
in a house	en una casa
in a flat	en un piso
I live with...	Vivo con...
I don't live with...	No vivo con...
my/your	mi, mis[1]/tu, tus[1]
family	la familia
parents	los padres
father/mother	el padre/la madre
stepfather	el padrastro
stepmother	la madrastra
husband/wife	el marido/la esposa
boyfriend	el novio
girlfriend	la novia
brother	el hermano
sister	la hermana
step brother	el hermanastro
step sister	la hermanastra
alone	solo/sola
single	soltero/soltera
married	casado/casada
surname	apellido
nickname	apodo
my address	mi dirección
my e-mail address	mi e-mail
Do you have e-mail?	¿Tienes e-mail?

[1] Use *mi* and *tu* with singular words, *mis* and *tus* with plural words.

37

Other people

¿Conoces a Carlos?
Do you know Carlos?

¿Quién es aquél?
Who's that?

Es muy divertido.
He's a good laugh.

Es alto.
He's tall.

Me gusta.
I like him/her.

Me cae fatal.
I can't stand him/her.

¿Qué le pasó a Paola?
What's happened to Paola?

¿Cómo es?
What's he/she like?

Nos llevamos bien.
We get on OK.

Ella no está mal.
She's quite pretty.

friend	un amigo/una amiga	**short**	bajo/baja
mate	un colega/una colega	**fat**	gordo/gorda
boy/girl	un chico/una chica	**thin**	delgado/delgada
someone	alguien	**fair**	rubio/rubia
has long hair	tiene el pelo largo	**dark**	moreno/morena
short hair	el pelo corto	**pretty**	guapa
curly hair	el pelo rizado	**is good-looking**[1]	está bueno/buena*
straight hair	el pelo liso	**isn't good-looking**[1]	no es guapo/guapa
has brown	tiene los ojos	**is OK (looks)**[1]	está bien
eyes	castaños	**ugly**	feo/fea
he/she is...	el/ella es...	**a bit, a little**	un poco
tall	alto/alta	**very**	muy

¿Conoces a alguien aquí?
Do you know anyone here?

¿Quieres tomar algo?
Do you want a drink?

¿Dame tu número de teléfono?
What's your phone number?

¿Quieres bailar?
Do you want to dance?

[1] There are two words for "is": *es* means "is (always)" e.g. *Es alto* (he is tall); *está* means "is (at the moment)" e.g. *Está de mal humor* (he is in a bad mood).

so	tan	an idiot	un/una idiota
really	realmente	in a bad mood	de mal humor
completely	completamente	in a good mood	de buen humor
nice, OK	simpático/simpática	hassled, annoyed	enfadado/enfadada
horrible, nasty	horrible	distressed	alterado
is cool, trendy[1]	está guay, está de moda	unhappy	disgustado
		depressed	deprimido/deprimida
is old-fashioned, geeky[1]	está anticuado/ anticuada	happy	contento
clever	listo/lista		
dim, stupid	burro/burra	**Have you heard that...?**	
boring	aburrido/aburrida	¿Sabes que...?	
shy	tímido/tímida		
mad, crazy	loco/loca	**Carlos is going out with Paola.**	
weird	raro/rara	Carlos está saliendo con Paola.	
lazy	perezoso/perezosa		
laid back	tranquilo/tranquila	**Juan fancies Maria.**	
up-tight	tenso/tensa	A Juan le gusta María.	
mixed up, untogether	confusa, hecha un lío		
		He/she kissed me.	
selfish	egoísta	Me besó.	
jealous	celoso/celosa		
rude	mal educado/educada	**They split up.**	
macho	machista	Han roto.	
a bit smooth	un poco falso/falsa		
stuck up	estirado, engreído	**We had a row.**	
cool	chulo/chula	Tuvimos una pelea./Nos peleamos.	
a creep	un pelotillero/una pelotillera		
		Leave me alone.	
		¡Déjame en paz!	

39

Sports

Catch!
¡Cógela!

In!/Out!
¡Dentro!/¡Fuera!

Throw it to me.
Tíramela.

Who won?
¿Quién ganó?

You're cheating!
¡Haces trampas!

How do you play this?
¿Cómo se juega?

What are the rules?
Explícame las reglas del juego.

What team do you support?
¿De qué equipo eres?

Is there a match we could go to?
¿Podríamos ir a ver algún partido?

Fact file

Spanish bull fighting is famous but it's not as popular as football. People play football, go to matches and watch it on TV, particularly in bars on Sunday evening. The big teams are *Real Madrid, F.C. Barcelona* and *Real Sociedad.* Tennis and basketball are popular. In the Basque country people play *pelota* (balls are hit against a wall with wicker rackets). There's an annual *Vuelta ciclista a España* (round Spain cycle race). Winter sports are becoming popular, with most resorts in the Pyrennes and the Sierra Nevada.

sport	un deporte	**tracksuit**	un chándal
match	un partido	**once a week**	una vez a la semana
a game (of)	una partida (de)	**twice a week**	dos veces a la semana
doubles	dobles		
singles	individuales	**I play...**	Juego al...
race	una carrera	**I don't play...**	No juego al...
marathon	un maratón	tennis	tenis
championships	unos campeonatos	squash	squash
Olympics	los juegos Olímpicos	badminton	bádminton
World Cup	La Copa del Mundo	football	fútbol
club	un club	American football	fútbol americano
team	un equipo	basketball	baloncesto
referee	un árbitro	volleyball	voleibol
supporter	un/una hincha	table tennis	tenis de mesa
training	entrenamiento	cricket	cricket
practice	práctica	baseball	béisbol
a goal	un gol	**I do/go...**	Hago...
to lose	perder	**I don't do/go...**	No hago...
to draw	empatar	judo	judo
sports centre	un centro de deportes	karate	kárate
stadium	un estadio	aerobics	aeróbic
gym	un gimnasio	weight-training	levantamiento de pesos
court	una pista		
indoor	cubierta	bowling	los bolos
outdoor	al aire libre	dancing	baile
ball	una pelota	yoga	yoga
net	una red	**I go jogging.**	Voy a correr.
trainers	unas zapatillas de deporte		

41

Sports

I like...	Me gusta...
I don't like...	No me gusta...
I love...	Me encanta...
I prefer...	Yo prefiero...
swimming	la natación
(scuba) diving	el submarinismo
sailing	la (navegación a) vela
surfing	hacer surf
water skiing	el esquí acuático
canoeing	el piragüismo
rowing	el remo
sunbathing	tomar el sol
boat	una barca
sail	la vela
surfboard	una tabla de surf
sea	el mar
beach	la playa
swimming pool	la piscina
in the sun	al sol
in the shade	a la sombra
mask	las gafas de bucear/de buceo
snorkel	el tubo
flippers	las aletas
wetsuit	el traje de neopreno
life jacket	el chaleco salvavidas
fishing	la pesca
fishing rod	la caña

cycling	el ciclismo
racing bike	una bici de carreras
mountain bike	una bici de montaña
touring bike	una bici de paseo
BMX	una bici BMX
horse riding	la equitación
horse	un caballo
walking, hiking	el senderismo
skateboard	un monopatín, un skateboard
roller skating	el patinaje sobre ruedas
ice rink	la pisaa de hielo
skates	los patines
skiing	el esquí
cross-country skiing	el esquí de fondo
snowboarding	snowboard
ski run	la pista
ski pass	el pase/el ticket
chair lift	el telesilla
drag lift	el telearrastre, el telesquí
skis	los esquíes
ski boots	las botas de esquiar
ski goggles	las gafas de esquiar
snow	la nieve

¿A qué hora acabas?
What time do you finish?

¿Tienes que trabajar mucho en casa?
Do you have a lot of work?

Si, cantidad.
Yes, loads.

I do...	Estudio...
computer studies	informática
maths	matemáticas, mates
physics	física
chemistry	química
biology	biología
natural sciences	ciencias naturales
geography	geografía
history	historia
economics	económicas
business studies	estudios empresariales
languages	idiomas
French	francés
English	inglés
Spanish	español
German	alemán
Italian	italiano
literature	literatura
philosophy	filosofía
sociology	sociología
religious studies	religión
general studies	estudios generales
design and technology	diseño y tecnología
art	arte
art history	historia del arte
drama	teatro
music	música
PE	educación física
school	un colegio, una escuela
boarding school	un internado
state education	enseñanza pública
private education	enseñanza privada
term	un trimestre
holidays	las vacaciones
beginning of term	el principio del trimestre

uniform	un uniforme
school club	un club
form leader	el encargado/la encargada
lesson, lecture	una clase
private lessons	clases particulares
conversation class	clase de conversación
homework	deberes
essay	un trabajo escrito
translation	una traducción
project	un proyecto
an option	una optativa
revision	un repaso
test	un exámen
oral test	un exámen oral
written	escrito
presentation	una exposición oral de un tema
continuous assessment	evaluación continua
mark, grade	nota
teacher	el profesor/la profesora
lecturer	el profesor/la profesora
(language) assistant	ayudante de conversación
good	bueno/buena
bad	malo/mala
strict	estricto/estricta
discipline	la disciplina
to repeat (a year)	repetir curso
to skive, to bunk off	pirar, hacer novillos
a grant	una beca
a loan	un préstamo
free	gratis

I'm a student.
Soy estudiante.

I'm still at school.
Aún voy a la escuela.

I want to do...
Quiero hacer...

He is skiving, bunking off.
Está haciendo novillos.

Fact file

Types of schools and colleges:
– *un colegio de enseñanza secundaria* (first stage of secondary school – for all pupils aged about 12 to 15)
– *un instituto de bachillerato* (second stage, 16 to 18 – similar to sixth form college)
– *una escuela de formación profesional* (as above, but with technical, vocational slant)
– *una universidad* (university)

School is compulsory until 16. State schools are mixed and there is no uniform. At each stage of secondary education the forms are called *primero, segundo* and *tercero*[1]. There is continuous assessment as well as a test for each subject every year. Anyone who fails has the option of retaking the test in September. At about 18 many pupils sit the *Selectividad*, the university entrance exam. Pupils have to travel to a university to sit this. Short-term degrees last three years, and lead to a *Diplomado* (a university diploma). Long-term degrees last up to six years, and lead to a *Licenciado*, or a professional degree.

¿Qué quieres hacer cuando acabes?
What do you want to do when you finish college?

¿Qué asignaturas haces?
What subjects are you doing?

¿Cuándo tienes los exámenes?
When are your exams?

¿En qué curso estás?
What year are you in?

¿Cuál te gusta más?
What do you like best?

[1]Literally, these mean first, second and third.

> *Trabajo en una tienda.*
> **I work in a shop.**

> *¿Qué tipo de actividades haces?*
> **What sort of things do you do?**

> *¿Tienes mucho tiempo libre?*
> **Do you get a lot of spare time?**

> *Me interesa mucho la fotografía.*
> **I'm interested in photography.**

> *Tengo un ordenador.*
> **I've got a PC.**

I do a lot of sport.	**I write poetry.**
Hago mucho deporte.	Escribo poesía.
I listen to a lot of music.	**I work in a café.**
Escucho muchísima música.	Trabajo en una cafetería.
I write songs.	**I do babysitting.**
Escribo canciones.	Trabajo de canguro.

> *¿Estás en internet?*
> **Are you on the internet?**

> *¿Qué teclas tengo que pulsar?*
> **What keys do I have to press?**

> *¿Qué hago ahora?*
> **What do I do now?**

> *¿A quién le toca?*
> **Whose go is it?**

I collect...	Colecciono...
stamps	sellos
all sorts of things	todo tipo de cosas
I like...	Me gusta...
drawing	dibujar
painting	pintar
acting	actuar
a part-time job	un trabajo a tiempo parcial
allowance, pocket money	la paga
computer	un ordenador
laptop	un ordenador portátil
software	software
computer games	juegos de ordenador
games consol	consola de juegos
word processing	procesamiento de textos
website	sitio web
disk	un disco
joystick	un mando
mouse	un ratón
game	un juego
chess	el ajedrez
board games	juegos de mesa
cards	las cartas
poker	el póquer
What are the rules?	¿Puedes explicarme las reglas del juego?

What do you want to do later?
¿Qué quieres hacer después?
When I finish...
Cuando acabe...
One day...
Un día...
I want to be a...
Quiero ser...

I want...
to live/work abroad
to travel
to have a career
to get a good job
to get my
  qualifications
to carry on studying

Quiero...
vivir/trabajar en el extranjero
viajar
tener una carrera
obtener un buen trabajo
obtener los títulos
  necesarios
continuar estudiando

What do you think about...?
¿Qué piensas sobre...?
I don't know much about...
No sé mucho sobre...
Can you explain...?
¿Puedes explicar...?
I feel angry about...
Me enfada que...

I think...
Creo que...
I belong to...
Soy de...
I believe in...
Creo en...
I don't believe in...
No creo en...

You're right.
Tienes razón.
I don't agree.
No estoy de acuerdo.
I'm for, I support...
Estoy a favor de...
I'm against...
Estoy en contra de...

the future	el futuro	**deforestation**	la desforestación
(in) the past	el pasado	**acid rain**	la lluvia ácida
now, nowadays	ahora	**nuclear power**	la energía nuclear
religion	la religión	**recycling**	el reciclaje
God	Dios	**politics**	la política
human rights	los derechos humanos	**government**	el gobierno
gay	gay	**democratic**	democrático/
feminist	feminista		democrática
abortion	el aborto	**elections**	las elecciones
drugs	las drogas	**party**	el partido
economy	la economía	**revolution**	la revolución
HIV	VIH positivo/positiva	**the left**	la izquierda
Aids	el sida	**the right**	la derecha
unemployment	el desempleo/el paro	**fascist**	fascista
Third World	el Tercer Mundo	**communist**	comunista
peace	la paz	**socialist**	socialista
war	la guerra	**greens, green**	los verdes
terrorism	el terrorismo	**movement**	
environment	el medio ambiente	**conservative**	conservador/
pollution	la contaminación		conservadora
conservation	la conservación	**politically**	políticamente,
global warming	calentamiento global	**active**	activo/activa
greenhouse effect	efecto invernadero	**march, demo**	una marcha, una
ozone layer	la capa de ozono		manifestación

Illness, problems, emergencies

It hurts a lot.	Duele mucho.
It hurts a little.	Duele un poco.
I've cut myself.	Me he cortado.
I think I've broken my...	Creo que me he roto...
My ... hurts	Me duele...
eye	el ojo
ear	el oído
I've been stung by a wasp.	Me ha picado una avispa.
I've got mosquito bites.	Tengo picaduras de mosquito.
He/She's had too much to drink.	Ha bebido demasiado.
I feel dizzy.	Me siento mareado/mareada.
I'm constipated.	Tengo estreñimiento.
I'm on medication for...	Estoy tomando medicamentos para...
I'm allergic to...	Soy alérgico/alérgica a...
antibiotics	los antibióticos
to some medicines	algunos medicamentos
I have...	Tengo...
food poisoning	una intoxicación
diarrhoea	diarrea
stomach cramp	una retortijón
muscle cramp	un calambre
sunstroke	una insolación
a headache	dolor de cabeza
a stomach ache	dolor de estómago
my period	el periodo
period pains	la regla*
an infection	una infección
a sore throat	dolor de garganta
a cold	un resfriado
flu	una gripe
a cough	una tos
hayfever	fiebre del heno
asthma	asma
a toothache	dolor de muelas
a temperature	fiebre
doctor	un doctor, un médico
female doctor	una doctora
dentist	un/una dentista
optician	un óptico/una óptica
chemist	una farmacia
pill	una pastilla
suppository[1]	un supositorio
injection	una inyección

No me encuentro bien.
I don't feel well.

¿Qué te pasa?
What's wrong?

Tengo ganas de vomitar.
I'm going to be sick.

Lo siento mucho.
I'm really sorry about this.

Quiero ir al médico.
I need to see a doctor.

¿Hay alguna farmacia abierta por aquí?
Is there a chemist open around here?

¿Puedes darme algo para fiebre del heno?
Can you give me something for hayfever?

[1]These are often prescribed in Spain.

Fact file

In Spain it's always advisable to carry proof of identity, so keep your passport with you. You may be asked to show your *papeles* (documents, ID). When carrying anything valuable or important, keep it out of sight.

For minor health problems or first aid treatment, go to a chemist. For something more serious go to a doctor. Look for an *Ambulatorio de la Seguridad Social* (local surgery). In an emergency go to a *Hospital de la Seguridad Social* (state-run hospital). In each case you should expect to pay. You should be able to claim back on insurance, but keep all the paperwork.

Emergencies

Emergency phone numbers:
all services 112; police 091;
ambulance 061 and fire brigade 080.

There's been an accident.	Ha habido un accidente.
Help!	¡Ayuda!
Fire!	¡Fuego!
Stop thief!	¡Al ladrón!
Please call...	Por favor, llame a...
an ambulance	una ambulancia
the police	la policía
the fire brigade	los bomberos

my wallet	mi cartera
(hand)bag	mi bolso
my things	mis cosas
my papers	mis papeles
my passport	mi pasaporte
my key	mi llave
my mobile	mi móvil
all my money	todo mi dinero
lost property	objetos perdidos
I'm lost.	Me he perdido.
I'm scared.	Tengo miedo.
I'm in trouble.	Tengo problemas.

I need to talk to someone.
Necesito hablar con alguien.

I don't know what to do...
No sé qué hacer...

I don't want to cause trouble, but...
No quiero molestar, pero...

A man's following me.
Un hombre me está siguiendo.

Can you keep an eye on my things?
¿Puedes vigilar mis cosas?

Has anyone seen...?
¿Alguien ha visto...?

Please don't smoke.
Por favor, no fume.

It doesn't work.
¡No funciona!

There's no water/power.
No hay agua/electricidad.

Slang and everyday Spanish

[1] If you're a boy, say *Estoy harto*.

This book has included informal Spanish and slang where appropriate, but these two pages list a few of the most common words and phrases.

When using slang it is easy to sound off-hand or rude without really meaning to. Here, as in the rest of the book, a single asterisk after a word shows that it is mild slang, so be careful how you use it.

Contractions and alternative pronunciations

How are you?	¿Qué tal? (Qué tal estás)
How are things?	¿Cómo va? (Cómo van las cosas?)
See you later.	Ta luego.* (Hasta luego.)
houses	casa* (casas)[1]
market	mercao* (mercado)
TV	la tele (televisión)

Abbreviations

teacher	el profe* (el profesor)
mate	el/la compa* (el compañero/ la compañera)
OK	vale

American and English imports

Un parking, un spot (**a commercial, an ad**), el look, sexy, stop, el estrés (**stress**), el corner (**in football**), el club, el marketing, el heavy metal, el estéreo, el cheque...

Fillers and exclamations

you know	sabes
well...	bien...
...er...	bueno
then	luego, entonces
Really?	¡Ah, sí?
Hey!	¡Vaya!

Wow!	¡Caray!
by the way	por cierto
I mean, that's to say	o sea
to mean something is "so so" or OK	psss
shows you agree or understand	ya, ya

Slang

great, fantastic	(ser)[2] guay* (ser) superguay*, (ser) bestial*
great, amazing	(ser)[2] alucinante*
very, hyper	super-, hiper-, ultra-
grotty	cutre*
good-looking	(estar)[2] bueno
geeky person	(ser)[2] un/una carca
parents	los viejos*
my boyfriend	mi chico*
my girlfriend	mi chica*, mi novia
friend, mate	un/una colega*
police	la pasma*
a bore, a pain	(ser)[2] un/una pelma un/una palizas* un/una plasta* un/una plomo* un/una peñazo* un muermo*
a flirt	(ser)[2] un ligón/una ligona*
stingy person	un/una rata*
skiver	un/una jeta*
thief	un chorizo/una choriza*
knowall	un enterado/una enterada
nutter	un chalado/una chalada*
job	un curro*
sandwich	un bocata*
jacket	una chupa*
a hassle	un lío
to steal, nick	robar, mangar*, birlar
to eat	papear*
to like	molar*
to be annoyed	estar cabreado/ cabreada*
to be low	estar depre*

[1] The plural "s" is often dropped in southern Spain. [2] Use with *ser* or *estar* (to be) as shown. See page 58.

Countries, nationalities, faiths

Countries

Africa	África	**country** el país	**continent** el continente
Asia	Asia	**north** el norte	**south** el sur
Australia	Australia	**east** el este	**west** el oeste
Austria	Austria		
Bangladesh	Bangladés		
Belgium	Bélgica		

Nationalities

You can say "I come from" + country:
e.g. *Soy de España*
or:
I am + adjective for nationality:
e.g. *Soy español/española*

Here are some common adjectives:

Brazil	Brasil
Canada	Canadá
Caribbean	El Caribe
Central America	Centroamérica
China	China
Dominica	Dominica
England	Inglaterra
Europe	Europa
France	Francia
Germany	Alemania
Great Britain	Gran Bretaña
Greece	Grecia
Hungary	Hungría
India	India
Ireland	Irlanda
Israel	Israel
Italy	Italia
Jamaica	Jamaica
Japan	Japón
Kenya	Kenia
Middle East	Oriente Medio
Mexico	México
Netherlands	Holanda
New Zealand	Nueva Zelanda
North Africa	África del Norte
Pakistan	Pakistán
Poland	Polonia
Portugal	Portugal
Russia	Rusia
Scandinavia	Escandinavia
Scotland	Escocia
South America	Sudamérica
Spain	España
Switzerland	Suiza
Tunisia	Túnez
Turkey	Turquía
United States	Estados Unidos
Vietnam	Vietnam
Wales	Gales

Adjectives column:

American	americano/americana
Australian	australiano/australiana
Austrian	austriaco/austriaca
Belgian	belga
Canadian	Canadiense
Dutch	holandés/holandesa
English	inglés/inglesa
French	francés/francesa
German	alemán/alemana
Indian	indio/india
Irish	irlandés/irlandesa
Italian	italiano/italiana
Pakistani	pakistaní
Scottish	escocés/escocesa
Spanish	español/española
Swiss	suizo/suiza
Welsh	galés/galesa

Faiths

agnostic	un agnóstico/ una agnóstica
atheist	un ateo/una atea
Buddhist	budista
Catholic	católico/católica
Christian	cristiano/cristiana
Hindu	hindú
Jewish	judío/judía
Muslim	musulmán/musulmana
Protestant	protestante
Sikh	sij

Numbers

0 cero	**30** treinta
1 uno[1]/una	**31** treinta y uno
2 dos	**40** cuarenta
3 tres	**50** cincuenta
4 cuatro	**60** sesenta
5 cinco	**70** setenta
6 seis	**71** setenta y uno
7 siete	**72** setenta y dos
8 ocho	**80** ochenta
9 nueve	**81** ochenta y uno
10 diez	**82** ochenta y dos
11 once	**90** noventa
12 doce	**91** noventa y uno
13 trece	**92** noventa y dos
14 catorce	**100** cien, ciento[2]
15 quince	**101** ciento uno
16 dieciséis	**200** dos cientos/cientas
17 diecisiete	**300** tres cientos/cientas
18 dieciocho	**1,000** mil
19 diecinueve	**1,100** mil cien
20 veinte	**1,200** mil dos cientos
21 veintiuno	**2,000** dos mil
22 veintidós	**2,100** dos mil cien
23 veintitrés	**10,000** diez mil
24 veinticuatro	**100,000** cien mil
25 veinticinco	**1,000,000** un millón

Colours

colour	color
light	claro
dark	oscuro
blue	azul
navy	azul marino
green	verde
yellow	amarillo/amarilla
orange	naranja
purple	morado/morada
pink	rosa
red	rojo/roja
white	blanco/blanca
grey	gris
brown	marrón
black	negro/negra

Days and dates

Monday	lunes
Tuesday	martes
Wednesday	miércoles
Thursday	jueves
Friday	viernes
Saturday	sábado
Sunday	domingo
January	enero
February	febrero
March	marzo
April	abril
May	mayo
June	junio
July	julio
August	agosto
September	septiembre
October	octubre
November	noviembre
December	diciembre
day	el día
week	la semana
month	el mes
year	el año
diary	una agenda
calendar	un calendario
yesterday	ayer
the day before yesterday	anteayer
today	hoy
the next day	el próximo día
tomorrow	mañana
the day after tomorrow	pasado mañana
last week	la semana pasada
this week	esta semana
next week	la semana próxima
What's the date?	¿Qué día es hoy?/ ¿A cuántos estamos?
on Mondays	los lunes
in August	en agosto
(on) 1st April	el uno de abril
in the year 2012	en el año dos mil doce

[1]*Uno* drops the "o" before masculine nouns, e.g. *un libro* (one book). [2]*Cien* changes into *ciento* when followed by a smaller number.

Time, seasons, weather, fact file: Spain and South America

Time

hour	hora
What time is it?	¿Qué hora es?
It's 1 o'clock.	Es la una.
It's 2 o'clock.	Son las dos.
minute	minuto
morning	la mañana
afternoon	la tarde
evening	la noche
midday	el mediodía
midnight	la medianoche
quarter past two	los dos y cuarto
half past two	los dos y media
quarter to two	las dos menos cuarto
five past two	las dos y cinco
ten to two	las dos menos diez
in ten minutes	dentro de diez minutos
half an hour ago	hace media hora
at 09:00	a las nueve
at 13:17	a las trece y diecisiete

Seasons and weather

season	la estación	**sky**	el cielo
spring	la primavera	**sun**	el sol
summer	el verano	**clouds**	las nubes
autumn	el otoño	**rain**	la lluvia
winter	el invierno	**snow**	la nieve

It's fine.	Hace buen tiempo.
It's sunny.	Hace sol.
It's hot.	Hace calor.
It's windy.	Hace viento.
It's raining.	Está lloviendo.
It's foggy.	Hay niebla.
It's snowing.	Está nevando.
It's icy.	Hay hielo.
It's cold.	Hace frío.
It's freezing.	Está helando.
It's horrible.	Hace un tiempo horrible.

What's the weather like?
¿Qué tiempo hace?

What's the weather forecast?
¿Cuál es el pronóstico del tiempo?

Fact file – Spain and South America

The Spanish that is used in this book is Castilian Spanish – the most widely spoken language in Spain. Outside of Spain, it is the language of most of South and Central America. This developed because of the widespread colonisation by Spain in the 16th and 17th century. Spain itself has four official national languages: Castilian, Catalan, Galician and Basque. The first three are all derived from Latin.

Castilian Spanish is spoken in the north, centre and south of Spain. Castilian itself has many dialects, which mainly involve differences in pronunciation. These occur in the Canary Islands and the south of Spain, in Andalucia, Extremadura and Murcia.

The Spanish of South and Central America (Latin American Spanish) developed originally from the Spanish of southern Spain. This is the area where the "c" is not lisped, as it is in most of Spain, and this along with some other local variations formed a basis for the language.

Catalan is spoken in the north-east of Spain – the area of Catalonia proper, coastal Valencia and the Balearic Islands (Majorca, Minorca and Ibiza). In these areas, Catalan is an official language alongside Castilian Spanish. It is taught in schools and widely spoken.

Galician is spoken in Galicia (in the north-west) along with Castilian Spanish. It is also spoken in parts of the neighbouring communities of Asturias and Castilla-Leon. Galician is very similar to Portuguese.

Basque is spoken in the Basque region (northern Spain).

Vowel sounds

In Spanish, vowel sounds are always short:

a sounds like "a" in "cat".

e sounds like "e" in "let".

i sounds like "i" in machine.

o sounds like "o" in "soft".

u sounds like "oo" in moon. It is silent after "q" and usually silent after "g" if it is followed by "e" or "i".

Groups of vowels

When in Spanish you have two or more vowels together, you usually pronounce each vowel in turn. For example, **eu** is said "e-oo" as in Europa, and **iu** is said "ee-oo", as in ciudad. The same applies to double vowels, for example **ee** is said "e-e" as in leer.

Consonants

c is hard as in "cat", except before "i" or "e" when it is like "th" in thumb.

ch sounds like the "ch" in "cheese".

d is like an English "d" except when it is on the end of a syllable. Then it is like "th" in "that".

g is like the "g" in "good" except before "e" or "i". Then it sounds like "ch" in the Scottish word "loch". When "g" is followed by "ue" or "ui", the "u" is not sounded but the "g" still sounds like the "g" in "good", for example in guerra and guitarra.

h is never pronounced.

j sounds like "ch" in the Scottish word "loch".

ll sounds like the "y" in "yes" but preceded by a hint of an "i".

ñ sounds like the "ni(o)" sound in "onion".

qu is the same sound as the hard "c" as in "cat".

r is a rolled or nearly trilled "r". Double "rr" sounds about the same. At the beginning of a word, "r" is strongly trilled, and on the end of a word it is not trilled quite so much.

v sounds like "b" in "big". There is no difference between a Spanish b and a Spanish v.

y sounds like "y" in "yes" when it is in the middle of a word. On the end of a word or on its own, e.g. *y* (and), it sounds like a Spanish *i* - like the "i" in "machine".

In Spanish you stress the last syllable of most words ending in a consonant. For words ending in a vowel, stress the second-to-last syllable. Any Spanish word that does not follow this pattern is written with a stress mark or accent. This shows you which part of the word you should stress, for example *árbol*.

The alphabet in Spanish

Applying the points made above, this is how you say the alphabet:
A, Be, Ce, CHe, De, E, eFe, Ge, Hache, I, Jota, Ka, eLe, eLLe, eMe, eNe, eÑe, O, Pe, Qu, eRe, eSe, Te, U, uVe, W=uve doble, X=equis, Y=igriega, Z=ceta.

How Spanish works

Nouns

All Spanish nouns are either masculine (m) or feminine (f). Nouns for people and animals have the obvious gender, e.g. *el padre* (father) and *el toro* (bull) are masculine and *la madre* (mother) and *la vaca* (cow) are feminine. For most nouns, though, the gender seems random, e.g. *autobús* (bus) is masculine and *casa* (house) is feminine. A few nouns can be either gender, e.g. *el/la turista* (tourist m/f).

The singular article (the word for "the" or "a") shows the noun's gender: with (m) nouns, "the" is *el*, e.g. *el autobús* (the bus) and "a" is *un*, e.g. *un autobus* (a bus); with (f) nouns, "the" is *la*, e.g. *la casa* (the house) and "a" is *una*, e.g. *una casa* (a house).

Don't worry if you muddle up *el* and *la*, you will still be understood. It is worth knowing the gender of nouns since other words, particularly adjectives, change to match them. If you're learning a noun, learn it with *el* or *la*. In general, nouns ending in "o" are masculine and those ending in "a" are feminine.

Plurals

In the plural, the Spanish for "the" is *los* + masculine noun and *las* + feminine noun, e.g. *los autobuses* (the buses), *las casas* (the houses).

Uno and *una* become *unos* and *unas*, e.g. *unos autobuses* (some buses), *unas casas* (some houses).

To make nouns plural, add "es" to any that end in a consonant, e.g *un tren, dos trenes* (a train, two trains) and add "s" to most nouns ending in a vowel, e.g. *un billete, dos billetes* (a ticket, two tickets).

A (to) and de (of, from)

In Spanish, "to" is *a*. When *a* precedes *el*, they contract to *al*, e.g. *Voy al mercado* (I'm going to the market).

The Spanish for "of" and "from" is *de*. When *de* precedes *el*, they join up and become *del*, e.g. *Soy del norte* (I'm from the north).

Spanish uses *de* to show possession where English does not, e.g. *el libro de Ana* (Ana's book), *el suéter del niño* (the kid's jumper).

Adjectives

In Spanish, most adjectives come after the noun they refer to, e.g. *la película larga* (the long film). They also agree with the noun – they change when used with a feminine or plural noun.

With feminine nouns, adjectives ending in "o" and a few others change to "a", e.g. *corto* becomes *corta*: *la novela corta* (the short novel). Others don't change, e.g. *feliz* (happy).

With plural nouns, most adjectives that end in a vowel have an "s", e.g *rojo* (m) becomes *rojos*: *los trenes rojos* (the red trains); *roja* (f) becomes *rojas*: *las camisetas rojas* (the red T-shirts). Those that end in a consonant have "es", e.g. *difícil* (difficult) becomes *difíciles*: *los exámenes difíciles* (the difficult exams).

Some common adjectives come before the noun, e.g. *gran* (big), *poco/poca* (little).

Making comparisons

To make a comparison, put the following words in front of the adjective: *más* (more, ...er), e.g. *más bonita* (prettier); *menos* (less), e.g. *menos bonita* (less pretty); *tan* (as), e.g. *tan bonita* (as pretty); *el/la más*

How Spanish works

(the most, the ...est), e.g. *la más bonita*
(the prettiest);
más ... que (more ... than, ...er ... than), e.g.
El es más alto que ella (he's taller than
her);
menos que (less ... than), e.g. *Ella es
menos alta que él* (she's less tall than
him);
tan ... como (as ... as), e.g. *El es tan
delgado como ella* (He's as thin as her).

There are exceptions, e.g. *bueno/buena*
(good), *mejor* (better), *el/la mejor* (the
best); *malo/mala* (bad), *peor* (worse), *el/la
peor* (the worst).

Very + adjective

Spanish has two ways of saying that
something is "very good/easy etc.". You
can use *muy* (very) + the adjective, e.g.
muy fácil (very easy), or the adjective +
-ísimo/ísima, e.g. *facilísimo/facilísima* (very
easy). Vowels on the end of the adjective
are dropped, e.g. *caro* (expensive),
carísimo (very expensive). This second
way is used a lot in colloquial Spanish.

Este/esta (this)

The Spanish for "this" is *este* + (m) noun,
e.g. *este chico* (this boy), *esta* + (f) noun,
e.g. *esta chica* (this girl), *estos* + plural (m)
noun, e.g. *estos chicos* (these boys), *estas*
+ plural (f) noun, e.g. *estas chicas* (these
girls).

Ese/esa, aquel/aquella (that)

There are two words for "that": *ese* when
the person or thing referred to is near the
person you're speaking to, e.g. who's that
guy on your right?, and *aquel* when the
person or thing is far from both of you,
e.g. that guy over there.
Ese and *aquel* change as follows: *ese* or
aquel + (m) noun, *esa* or *aquella* + (f)

noun; *esos* or *aquellos* + plural (m) noun;
esas or *aquellas* + plural (f) noun.

I, you, he, she etc.

Spanish often leaves out "I", "you", etc. The
verb changes according to who or what is
doing the action (see Verbs, page 58) so
they are not needed, e.g. *Estoy pensando*
(I am thinking, literally "am thinking"); *Es
un bar* (It's a bar, literally "Is a bar"). It
helps to know these words as the verb
has various forms to correspond to each
of them.

I *yo*

you *tú, usted, vosotros/-as, ustedes*

There are four words for "you": *tú* is
singular informal; say tú to a friend or
someone your own age or younger. *Usted,*
often writted *Ud.,* is singular polite (pol.).
Use it to a person you don't know or you
want to show respect to (someone older);
Vosotros/-as is plural informal, (m)/(f). Use
it like *tú* but when speaking to more than
one person. Use *vosotras* when talking to
girls or women only; *ustedes* (written *Uds.*)
is plural polite (pl.pol.). Use it like *usted*
but for more than one person. If in doubt,
use the polite forms.

he *él*   **she** *ella*   **it** *él/ella*
There's no special word for "it". The verb is
used on it's own.

we *nosotros/-as*
Nosotros means "we" for males or males
and females, *nosotras* means "we" for
females only.

they *ellos/ellas*
Ellos is for males, *ellas* for females.

How Spanish works

My, your, his, her etc.

These words agree with the noun they relate to, e.g. *mi hermano* (my brother), *mis padres* (my parents), *nuestra casa* (our house) etc:

In front of singular noun		plural noun
my	mi	mis
your	tu	tus
his/her/its, your (pol.)	su	sus
our	nuestro/-a	nuestros/-as
your	vuestro/-a	vuestros/-as
their, your (pl.pol.)	su	sus

Verbs

Spanish verbs have more tenses (present, future, simple past etc.) than English verbs, but there are simple ways of getting by which are explained here.

Present tense

Spanish verbs end in "ar", "er" or "ir" in the infinitive[1], e.g. *comprar* (to buy), *comer* (to eat), *escribir* (to write), and follow one of these three patterns. Drop "ar", "er", or "ir" and replace it with the ending you need:

to buy	compr ar
I buy	compr o
you buy	compr as
he/she/it buys, you buy (pol.)	compr a
we buy	compr amos
you buy	compr áis
they buy, you buy (pl.pol.)	compr an

to eat	com er
I eat	com o
you eat	com es
he/she/it eats, you eat (pol.)	com e
we eat	com emos
you eat	com éis
they eat, you eat (pl.pol.)	com en

to write	escribir
I write	escrib o
you write	escrib es
he/she/it writes, you write (pol.)	escribe
we write	escrib imos
you write	escrib ís
they write, you write (pl.pol.)	escrib en

Spanish verbs are mostly used without "I", "you" etc. (see I, you, he, she etc. on page 57). It helps to learn them as a list, e.g. *como, comes* etc.

Spanish doesn't distinguish as much as English between present (I write) and present continuous (I'm writing). Unless you want to stress that the action is happening now (e.g. He's sleeping), the present tense is used, e.g. *Viene hoy* (she is coming today, literally "she comes today").

Ser and estar (to be)

Spanish has two verbs "to be". *Ser* is used to describe people and things, e.g. *Soy inglés* (I am English), *Es camarero* (He's a waiter), and to tell the time, e.g. *Son las tres* (It's three). *Estar* is for saying where people and things are, e.g. *Está lejos* (It's far) and describing anything changeable or short-lived, e.g. *Está de mal humor* (He's in a bad mood). Both are irregular:

to be	ser	estar
I am	soy	estoy
you are	eres	estás
he/she/it is, you are (pol.)	es	está
we are	somos	estamos
you are	sois	estáis
they are, you are (pl.pol.)	son	están

[1]The infinitive is the form in which verbs are given in dictionaries.

Other useful irregular verbs

to have	**tener**
I have	*tengo*
you have	*tienes*
he/she/it has, you have (pol.)	*tiene*
we have	*tenemos*
you have	*tenéis*
they have, you have (pl.pol.)	*tienen*

to go	**ir**
I go	*voy*
you go	*vas*
he/she/it goes, you go (pol.)	*va*
we go	*vamos*
you go	*vais*
they go, you go (pl.pol.)	*van*

to do	**hacer**
I do	*hago*
you do	*haces*
he/she/it does, you do (pol.)	*hace*
we do	*hacemos*
you do	*hacéis*
they do, you do (pl.pol.)	*hacen*

to be able to (can)	**poder**
I can	*puedo*
you can	*puedes*
he/she/it can, you can (pol.)	*puede*
we can	*podemos*
you can	*podéis*
they can, you can (pl.pol.)	*pueden*

Stem-changing verbs

These are verbs whose stem (the part before the "ar", "er", or "ir" ending) changes as well as the endings. These three are especially useful:

to want	**querer**
I want	*quiero*
you want	*quieres*
he/she/it wants, you want (pol.)	*quiere*
we want	*queremos*
you want	*queréis*
they want, you want (pl.pol.)	*quieren*

to prefer	**preferir**
I prefer	*prefiero*
you prefer	*prefieres*
he/she/it prefers, you prefer (pol.)	*prefiere*
we prefer	*preferimos*
you prefer	*preferís*
they prefer, you prefer (pl.pol.)	*prefieren*

to play	**jugar**
I play	*juego*
you play	*juegas*
he/she/it plays, you play (pol.)	*juega*
we play	*jugamos*
you play	*jugáis*
they play, you play (pl.pol.)	*juegan*

Reflexive verbs

Spanish has far more reflexive verbs than English. They all have "se" infinitive[1] endings, e.g. *lavarse* (to get washed/wash oneself), *levantarse* (to get up, literally "to get oneself up").

Here is the present of a common one:

I get up	*me levanto*
you get up	*te levantas*
he/she/it gets up, you get up (pol.)	*se levanta*
we get up	*nos levantamos*
you get up	*os levantáis*
they get up, you get up (pl.pol.)	*se levantan*

How Spanish works

Talking about the future

"Ar", "er" and "ir" verbs (see present tense) all have the same endings in the future tense:

I shall buy	comprar é
you will buy	comprar ás
he/she/it will buy, you will buy (pol.)	comprar á
we will buy	comprar emos
you will buy	comprar éis
they will buy, you will buy (pl.pol.)	comprar án

Another future tense is made with the present of *ir* (to go) + a + the verb's infinitive, e.g. *Voy a comprar* (I'm going to buy). It is used for something that is just about to happen.

Talking about the past

The most useful past tense in Spanish is the simple past tense. "Ar" verbs have one set of endings and "er" and "ir" verbs have another:

to buy	compr ar
I bought	compr é
you bought	compr aste
he/she/it bought, you bought (pol.)	compr ó
we bought	compr amos
you bought	compr ásteis
they bought, you bought (pl.pol.)	compr aron

to eat	com er
I ate	com í
you ate	com iste
he/she/it ate, you ate (pol.)	com ió
we ate	com imos
you ate	com ísteis
they ate, you ate (pl.pol.)	com ieron

The past tenses of "to be" and "to do" are also useful:

to be	ser	estar
I was	fui	estuve
you were	fuiste	estuviste
he/she/it was, you were (pol.)	fue	estuvo
we were	fuimos	estuvimos
you were	fuísteis	estuvísteis
they were, you were (pl.pol.)	fueron	estuvieron

The past tense of *ir* (to go) is the same as the past tense of *ser*, so *fui* can also mean "I went", *fue* (he/she/it went), *fuimos* (we went) etc.

to do	hacer
I did	hice
you did	hiciste
he/she/it did, you did (pol.)	hizo
we did	hicimos
you did	hicisteis
they did, you did (pl.pol.)	hicieron

Negatives

To make a sentence negative, put *no* in front of the verb, e.g. *No comprendo* (I don't understand), *No me levanto* (I don't get up).

Other useful negative words include *nunca* (never), *nadie* (noboby), *nada* (nothing), *ninguno/ninguna* (any).

Making questions

To make a question, just give a sentence the intonation of a question – raise your voice at the end. Questions can begin with words like:

who?	¿quién?	how?	¿cómo?
what?	¿qué?	where?	¿dónde?
when?	¿cuándo?	how much?	¿cuánto/ cuánta?
which? what?	¿cuál?		

This list gives you some useful words that will help you to get by in Spanish. Adjectives with two forms are given twice: (m) followed by (f) (see page 56) and verbs are given in the infinitive.

accident	el accidente
address	la dirección
in advance	por adelantado
after	después
afternoon	la tarde
against	en contra de, contra
age	edad
to agree	estar de acuerdo
airport	el aeropuerto
alone	solo/sola
ambulance	la ambulancia
and	y
animals	los animales
another	otro/otra
anyone	alguien
to arrive	llegar
to ask	preguntar
bad	malo/mala
bag	la bolsa
ball	la pelota
bank	el banco
bath	la bañera
bathroom	el cuarto de baño
to be	ser, estar
beach	la playa
beautiful	bonito/bonita
because	porque
behind	detrás
to believe	creer
beware	tener cuidado
bicycle	la bicicleta
big	grande
bill	la cuenta
birthday	cumpleaños
boat	el barco, la barca
book	el libro
to book, reserve	reservar
booking	la reserva
boring	aburrido
bottle	la botella
boy	el niño
bread	el pan
to break	romper, romperse
to breakdown	una avería
breakfast	el desayuno
bridge	el puente
brilliant	fantástico
brother	el hermano
bus	el autobús
bus station	la estación de autobuses
bus stop	la parada de autobús
busy	ocupado/ocupada

butter	la mantequilla
to buy	comprar
bye	adiós, hasta la vista
café	el café
cake	el pastel
to call	llamar
to camp	acampar
camping	el camping
to cancel	cancelar
car	el coche
to carry	llevar
cashier's desk	la caja
castle	el castillo
to catch	attrapar, coger
cathedral	la catedral
chair	la silla
to change	cambiar
cheap	barato/barata
cheese	el queso
chocolate	el chocolate
church	la iglesia
close	cerca
closed	cerrado/cerrada
clothes	la ropa
coffee	el café
cold	frío/fría
colour	color
to come	venir
completely	completamente
to confirm	confirmar
cool	guay
to cost	costar
countryside	el campo
to cross	cruzar
crossroads	el cruce de carreteras
customs	la aduana
dangerous	peligroso/peligrosa
day	el día
delay	el retraso
delicious	muy bueno/buena
department store	los grandes almacenes
dessert	el postre
dictionary	el diccionario
difficult	difícil
dinner	la cena
to do	hacer
doctor	el doctor/la doctora
downstairs	abajo
drink	la bebida
to drink	beber
drinking water	agua potable
easy	fácil
to eat	comer
eggs	los huevos
end of, at the end	al final
English	inglés
enough	suficiente
entrance	la entrada

evening	la tarde, la noche	last	último/última
every day	diario/diaria	later	después
except	excepto	latest	último/última
excuse me	perdone/perdona, por favor	to learn	aprender
		to leave (depart)	salir
exit	la salida	to leave (a message)	dejar
to expect	esperar	left	izquierda
expensive	caro/cara	lemon	el limón
to explain	explicar	less	menos
		library	la biblioteca
family	la familia	to like	gustar
far	lejos	to listen	escuchar
father	el padre	a little	un poco
to finish	terminar	to live	vivir
first	primero/primera	long	largo/larga
fish	el pescado	to look	mirar
fork	el tenedor	to look for	buscar
friend	el amigo/la amiga	to lose	perder
fruit	la fruta	lost	perdido/perdida
full	completo/completa	loud	alto/alta
		lunch	la comida
girl	la chica		
glass	el vaso	Madam, Mrs.	señora
glasses	las gafas	main course	el segundo plato
to go	ir	make-up	el maquillaje
good	bueno/buena	man	el hombre
goodbye	adiós	map	el mapa
guide book	la guía	market	el mercado
		maybe	quizás
hair	el pelo	meal	la comida
happy	feliz	meat	la carne
to have	tener	medicines	los medicamentos
to hear	oír	to meet	encontrarse
heavy	pesado/pesada	menu	el menú
hello	hola	milk	la leche
to help	ayudar	mineral water	el agua mineral
here	aquí	Miss	señorita
Hi!	¡Hola!	money	el dinero
hospital	el hospital	month	el mes
hot	calor/caliente	more	más
hotel	el hotel	morning	la mañana
house	la casa	mother	la madre
how?	¿cómo?	Mr., Sir	señor
hungry	hambre	Mrs., madam	señora
husband	el marido	museum	el museo
		music	la música
important	importante		
ill	enfermo/enferma	name	nombre
in front of	delante de	near (to)	cerca
interesting	interesante	nearby	cerca de aquí
		new	nuevo/nueva
jacket	la chaqueta	news	las noticias
jam	la mermelada	newspapers	los periódicos
job	el trabajo	next	próximo/próxima
journey	el trayecto	nice (referring to people)	simpático/simpática
key	la llave	night	la noche
kind (type)	tipo	no	no
knife	el cuchillo	no-one	nadie
to know	saber, conocer	now, nowadays	ahora
large	grande	number	el número

OK	bien	seat	el asiento
old	viejo/vieja	to see	ver
one way	dirección única	to see again	ver otra vez
open	abierto/abierta	see you soon	hasta pronto
opposite	en frente de	to sell	vender
or	o	shampoo	el champú
to order	pedir	shops	las tiendas
other	otro/otra	short	corto/corta, bajo/baja
outdoor	al aire libre	to show	indicar
over	sobre	shower (bathroom)	la ducha
		to be sick	vomitar
passport	el pasaporte	to sing	cantar
(in) the past	el pasado	Sir, Mr.	señor
pasta	la pasta	sister	la hermana
path, footpath	la senda, el camino	size	la talla
to pay	pagar	to sleep	dormir
people	la gente	small	pequeño/pequeña
pepper	la pimienta	snow	la nieve
pharmacy	la farmacia	so	tan
phone	teléfono	soap	el jabón
picnic	el picnic, la excursión	someone	alguien
plate	el plato	something	algo
platform	el andén	song	la canción
to play	jugar	sorry	perdone/perdona
please	por favor	soup	la sopa
police	la policía	to speak	hablar
postbox	el buzón	spoon	la cuchara
postcard	la postal	square	la plaza
post office	la oficina de correos,	stairs	la escalera
	correos	stamp	el sello
to prefer	preferir	to start	empezar
pretty	guapa	starter	el primer plato
price	el precio	(train) station	la estación
to put	poner	to stay	estar
		straight ahead	todo recto
quite	bastante	street	la calle
		strong	fuerte
radio	la radio	student	el/la estudiante
rain	la lluvia	to study	estudiar
to read	leer	sugar	el azúcar
really	realmente	sun	el sol
to repair	arreglar	sunglasses	gafas de sol
replacement	repuesto	sunscreen	la crema con protección
to reserve	reservar		total
restaurant	el restaurante	supermarket	el supermercado
right	derecha	surname	apellido
to be right	tener razón	sweet (taste)	dulce
river	el río	to swim	nadar
road	la carretera	swimming pool	la piscina
room	la habitación		
rude	mal educado/educada	table	la mesa
rules	las reglas	to take	tomar
to run	correr	tall	alto/alta
		taxi	el taxi
sad	triste	tea	el té
salad	la ensalada	teacher	el profesor/la profesora
salt	la sal	telephone	teléfono
to say	decir	to tell	decir
to say again, repeat	repetir	thank you	gracias
school	el conejo, la escuela	there	allí
sea	el mar	things	cosas

to throw	tirar, lanzar	to wake up	despertarse
ticket	el billete, la entrada	to walk	pasear, andar
time	tiempo, la hora	to want	querer
timetable	el horario	to wash	lavar
tired	cansado/cansada	water	agua
tissues	los pañuelos de papel	weather	el tiempo
today	hoy	week	la semana
toilet	el lavabo, los servicios	weird	raro/rara
tomorrow	mañana	what?	¿qué?
tonight	esta noche	when?	¿cuándo?
too	demasiado, también	where?	¿dónde?
town	la ciudad	why?	¿por qué?
town hall	el ayuntamiento	wife	la esposa
train	el tren	with	con
to try	intentar	woman	la mujer
to try on	probar	work	trabajar
to turn	girar	to write	escribir
TV	la televisión		
		year	el año
ugly	feo/fea	yes	sí
under	debajo	yesterday	ayer
university	la universidad	young	joven
very	muy	zip	la cremallera
village	el pueblo		

Index

If you can't find the phrasebook section you want from the Contents page, try looking here.

accommodation, 12-15
adjectives, 4, 56
air travel, 10
alphabet, 55

banks, 16-17
Basque, 54
bed and breakfast, 12
beliefs, 47, 52
books, 34-35
bus travel, 8-9

cafés, 18-19, 21
camping, 12, 24
Castilian, 54
Catalan, 54
clothes, 28-29
colours, 53
countries, 52
cycling, 11

dates (calendar), 53
days of the week, 53
directions, asking for, 6-7
drink words, 18-19

emergencies, 49

entertainment, 32, 33

faiths 52
films, 33, 34-35
food
  shopping, 24, 25, 27
  words, 18-23, 24, 25, 27

Galician, 54
grammar, 56-60

hotels, 13

illness, 48-49
interests, 46-47
issues, 46-47

money, 16-17
months, 53
music, 30-31

nationalities, 52
negative sentences, 60
nouns, 56
numbers, 53

phoning, 15, 17
plurals, 56
politeness, 4, 14, 57
politics, 47
post offices, 16-17
pronunciation, 4, 55

restaurants, 20-21
road travel, 6-7, 11

sea travel, 10
school, 44-45
seasons, 54
shopping, 24-29
sightseeing, 6-7, 32-33
slang, 4, 50-51
socializing, 32-39, 46
South America, 54
sports, 40-43
studying, 44-45

taxis, 10
television, 34-35
time, 54
tourist information, 6, 12
train travel, 8-9
travel, 8-11

underground travel, 8-9

verbs, 58-60

weather, 54

"you", familiar and polite
  forms, 4, 57
youth hostels, 12